# THE KINEMA IN THE WOODS

## THE STORY OF WOODHALL SPA'S UNIQUE CINEMA

by
**Edward Mayor**

For Eva Allport and her family,
and all who have worked in the Kinema.

Published by J. W. Green Cinemas, 2002

**To mark the occasion of the
Kinema's Eightieth Anniversary.**

First Published 2002

Copyright © Edward R. Mayor

ISBN: 0-9543037-0-9

**Cover Photographs**

Front cover: (top) the Kinema in the early 'thirties
(below) as it is today, with Kinema Too on the left.

Back cover: The Compton Kinestra organ displayed in the
Kinema foyer shortly before its installation in 1987.

All rights reserved. No part of this book may be reproduced,
stored in a retrieval system, nor transmitted in any form by any means,
electronic, mechanical, photocopying, whether recording or otherwise,
without the prior permission in writing of the copyright holders
or their authorised agents.

Origination and Printing by F. W. Cupit (Printers) Ltd
The Ropewalk, 23 Louth Road, Horncastle, Lincolnshire LN9 5ED

# Acknowledgements

It is a great pleasure to record my thanks to the people mentioned below, and to thank those who wish to remain anonymous but whose help has been invaluable.

James Green, the owner of the Kinema, suggested the project and has from the outset supplied a lot of material, enabling me to examine the deeds which were kindly loaned by Chattertons of Horncastle.

Mrs Eva Allport has been most generous with her time and her memories, as have Mrs Maureen Avison, Mrs Dorothy Bycroft, Amy Dulake, Mrs Mildred Matthews, Mrs Jean Stollery, Mr Gordon Allport, Mr Stan Cerklewicz, Messrs. Hugh and Robert Croft, Mr Tim Curtis, Leonard E. Field, Mr Terry Hodson, Mr Neil Hotchkin, Mr Peter Osborne, Mr Peter Pendlebury and Mr Alan Underwood.

Mr David Hill kindly prepared the specification of the Kinema's Compton organ especially for this book.

The staff of the following places have been very kind: Horncastle Library, Woodhall Spa Library, The Cottage Museum Woodhall Spa and its Trustees, The Horncastle News and the Kinema in the Woods.

Recorded memories of those who are no longer with us have been invaluable, including those of Miss Sheila Bycroft, Mrs Beatrice Dulake, and Mrs Ellen Webb. The film director Mr Bryan Forbes and the late Mr Bill Skelton have also recorded many useful memories.

Finally I am very grateful to Amy Dulake who put the text onto computer, and James Green. Together they ensured that events of the last thirty years received their due in the text, and their good humour and enthusiasm underpinned all our work. I hope that what follows will pay tribute to their dedication and the dedication of their staff, who make a night out at the Kinema so special.

*Edward R. Mayor*
*May 2002*

Copyright © Edward R. Mayor

## Foreword

This book crystallises a unique history, a history of determination, local endeavour, flair, and above all, vision. The Kinema is a place where the modern world is constantly taken on board then given a firmly traditional dusting, an enterprise where old values hold fast. The spirit of the Kinema, under the inspired guidance of Lady Weigall, Major Allport and now James Green, leaps out from the following pages. Fascinating details reveal to the humble reader from whence came the name and nicknames, the splendid Compton Kinestra organ, the exquisite trompe l'oeil painting, the contribution to the War years and all the many ingredients, which make up Lincolnshire's finest and most unique cinema.

Neither neon lighting nor scent of popcorn leap out to meet the eager patron bent upon an evening's entertainment, but a warm welcome, providing the distinctive feeling that the Kinema is a place like no other. Halfway through the film, a halt is called, sometimes at a pregnant moment, when the lights (oh! the joy of those splendid art deco lights in Kinema Too!) come to life and it is interval time – in similar vein to the early days when films were shown in serial form with the viewer left bound in suspense for next week's installment. And should you need just another minute or two to finish your ice cream, whilst perchance the smokers are collected from outside, then the time is yours before the film recommences and the agony of drama is 'once again' released.

We learn how the Kinema extends itself well beyond the expected showing of current films; indeed one of our own best memories is the 50th Anniversary celebration of the end of the 2nd World War in Europe. Dressed up '40's style with our children, we became immersed in the atmosphere that evening at the Kinema watching a Pathé News reel between showings of **The Dambusters** and **Dad's Army**. And we remembered with grateful thanks the many brave RAF fighter pilots long since passed who sat in Kinema seats years before, and who did so much to preserve us.

This is a very important history of a living Lincolnshire landmark, expertly penned by local author Edward Mayor, and all contributors are to be commended for the details and the joy this work will provide.

*Francis and Rosalie Dymoke*
*Scrivelsby, June 2002*

# Contents

The reels of the silent movies had to be changed every ten minutes, therefore;

Reel One: If You Go Down in the Woods Today . . . . . . . . . . . . . . . . . . . 6

Reel Two: A Pavilion in the Mists of Time . . . . . . . . . . . . . . . . . . . . . . . 9

Reel Three: A Very Shaky Start . . . . . . . . . . . . . . . . . . . . . . . . . . . . 22

Reel Four: Allport In Charge . . . . . . . . . . . . . . . . . . . . . . . . . . . . . . 25

Reel Five: Lured By Chocolates . . . . . . . . . . . . . . . . . . . . . . . . . . . . 34

Reel Six: The Talkies Take Over . . . . . . . . . . . . . . . . . . . . . . . . . . . . 36

Reel Seven: Conflict and Resolution . . . . . . . . . . . . . . . . . . . . . . . . . 38

Reel Eight: The Flicks in the Sticks . . . . . . . . . . . . . . . . . . . . . . . . . . 49

Reel Nine: Allport Soldiers On . . . . . . . . . . . . . . . . . . . . . . . . . . . . . 53

Reel Ten: New Era, New Facilities . . . . . . . . . . . . . . . . . . . . . . . . . . 57

Reel Eleven: Kinema Too and Future Plans . . . . . . . . . . . . . . . . . . . . . 71

Reel Twelve: Down Memory Lane . . . . . . . . . . . . . . . . . . . . . . . . . . . 74

Appendix i: Specification of the Compton Kinestra organ . . . . . . . . . . . . 78
*prepared by David Hill*

Appendix ii: The projection Equipment . . . . . . . . . . . . . . . . . . . . . . . 80
*A note by James Green*

## REEL 1
## *If you go down in the woods today....*

No matter which way you approach it, the Kinema in the Woods plays hide and seek, and when you finally discover the half timbered "Hansel and Gretel" building with its fairy lights, which would look at home in an Alpine forest village, you may wonder whether you are awake or dreaming.

The Kinema has shown films continually since September 1922, closing only briefly for refurbishments. Eye-witness accounts enable us to evoke the excitement of a night out at this dream palace of the "Roaring Twenties" as the decade draws to a close.

It is little Rosa's tenth birthday, and Mummy and Daddy are treating her to a night out at the pictures. Usually she would perch on the benches at the back, with her young friends, but tonight she has been allowed to sit in one of the best seats on the front row. It may seem strange, but these seats are deck chairs, wider than those at the seaside and so comfortable with their cushions and antimacassars which are laundered each week. The audience is settling down, but Rosa notices that the deck chairs at her side are still empty.

The buzz of conversation becomes a flurry of hushed remarks as someone whispers "They're here!" Rosa looks round to see a group of people in evening dress being welcomed by a man in tails, who bows low to one person in particular, a slim lady in satin and furs.

The group of gorgeously dressed people moves slowly down towards the deck chairs. The audience is now silent. A lady on crutches accompanies the one in furs, and is transferred into a wicker armchair with hastily plumped-up cushions. She turns to the audience and smiles, revealing a pearl necklace and diamonds which flash and fascinate.

The film show should have begun a full ten minutes ago, but Rosa's attention has been absorbed by this cavalcade settling into their deckchairs. In fact, the lady in furs has now seated herself in the very next deckchair and has produced a large box of chocolates which she smilingly offers to Rosa. Imagine her surprise when Daddy whispers that this is none other than Her Royal Highness the Princess Marie Louise, grand-daughter of Queen Victoria! The other people are Viscounts, Earls, Lords and all their Ladies, each of whom are offered a chocolate in their turn.

Rosa realises that the lady on crutches once invited her to perch on the back seat of her motorised wheel chair and took her for a ride around the gardens of nearby Petwood House. Yes, this is Lady Grace Weigall, who loves children, parties and fun, and who brought the cinema to Woodhall Spa.

A sudden roll on the drums is played by a man in the orchestra pit and the house lights are switched off. All eyes go to the screen, which is surrounded by posh curtains gathered in swags. A rather intense lady seated at the piano begins to whip the keys into a fury as the flickering titles roll on the silent film. Every sound from the piano matches the actions on the screen. Warmed by the glowing heat from the huge iron coke-stoves, little Rosa sinks back into her shilling deck chair. She has entered the land of dreams, and tonight, Buster Keaton's antics will bring the house down.

Now, this may sound like a fairy-tale, but every detail is true. Royalty, aristocracy and the general public really did share an evening out at the cinema in the Woodhall Spa of the 1920's. Princess Marie Louise was still there in the 'thirties and so was Lord Clydesdale who flew over Everest and watched his achievements on film. But there were a number of practical problems associated with the conversion of a former cricket pavilion and concert hall into a cinema. The parallel beams supporting the roof were too low to enable a projection room to show films from the rear of the audience, and would have got in the way of the beams from the projector. So a corrugated iron hut was added at the back of the stage, and projectors threw the image for some thirty feet onto the back of a special linen screen, kept damp so that it would be translucent.

The image on this screen was very sharp, meaning that the best seats — deck chairs — were at the front.

There were originally no toilets inside the cinema, so anyone needing to "spend a penny" had to be taken, usually by a willing youngster, to public conveniences beyond the bandstand opposite the Spa Baths.

Often, customers in the deck chairs were kicked in the rear when someone behind them decided to uncross their legs. Having been on the receiving end once too often, Princess Marie Louise had to ask the proprietor, Captain Allport, if she could have a deck chair situated where she could avoid being kicked!.

It is a matter of debate locally whether Lady Weigall and her guests really did keep the audience waiting, but a majority maintain that she did, and all agree that the show could not start until her party was seated.

How and why did this most unusual cinema materialise in Woodhall Spa? The Weigalls had returned from south Australia in early June 1922. Sir Archibald had been Governor there, a royal appointment, and he and Lady Weigall had resided in Adelaide. On their return to Petwood House, they found the Spa and Baths in crisis. Visitors had dwindled after the First World War, which had wiped out a whole way of life. The Weigalls set about reviving the Spa Baths and working with the Hotchkins, the Lords of the Manor, to improve amenities. The Pavilion Cinema was part of this plan. The year 1922 also saw the birth of the BBC, the rise to fame of cinema idols Rudolph Valentino and Ramon Navarro, and the discovery of Tutankhamen's tomb in Egypt. Lady Weigall was susceptible to handsome men of stage and screen, and no doubt wanted to divert her many aristocratic and theatrical friends with the latest films featuring the new movie stars. She sent a letter to the Horncastle News published on Saturday September 9th, announcing her new cinema as an experiment, and inviting local support:

> "The neighbourhood has for some time felt the need for this form of entertainment", she said, and thus it was that on Monday September 11th at 7pm, a picturesque pavilion opened its front doors for the first time as the Pavilion Cinema. The rest, as they say, is history.

# REEL 2
## A Pavilion in the Mists of Time

It all began in 1811 when men working for the local land owner John Parkinson discovered water in a mine shaft he had originally sunk in the hope of finding coal. The water was not analysed for many years, but when it was, its potential for healing was recognised. Uniquely, it contained equal quantities of Bromine and Iodine. The discovery in Coal Pit Wood was to change this sandy flatland into one of England's Spa Towns, named after the nearby hamlet of Old Woodhall. To this end, Thomas Hotchkin purchased the land from Parkinson and built, between 1844-5, a Bath House and an hotel at the huge cost of £30,000.

The hotel was appropriately named The Victoria and it eventually attracted many titled people whose names were listed weekly in the local papers. Nestling in its own wooded grounds and with its own bandstand, it looked out upon land which was part woodland and part heath, crossed by streams. This land had obviously been developed by the 1860's, for a letter of January 1st 1862 to Stafford Hotchkin confirms that a certain Thomas Wells was willing to take "Woodhall Spa Hotel and Bath House, Pump Room, Stabling, Offices and Outbuildings, Pleasure and Garden Ground, Archery and Cricket Ground on lease for 21 years at a rent of £150 for the first two years and afterwards at £200 per annum".

Stafford Hotchkin refurbished the hotel in 1884 and sold 75 acres including hotel and bath house to a syndicate of influential men in 1887. The Rev. J. O. Stephens of Blankney masterminded this syndicate, which included three Members of Parliament: Edward Stanhope, Sir Richard Webster, and the Rt Hon. H Chaplin. They made improvements to the hotel and grounds and installed automatic machinery for the Spa well. The land became known as the Spa Pleasure Grounds and on Saturday July 14th 1888 we read the first printed accounts of a pavilion, no doubt built by the syndicate. Reporting on a vast Fete in the Pleasure Grounds, the Horncastle News said:

*"There has been erected in the grounds a spacious pavilion where dancing and other amusements can be indulged in."*

This could have been the pavilion which eventually became the Kinema, for "erected" tends to suggest a wooden structure. A "pastoral play" called "King Rene's Daughter" was staged in this pavilion by the Horncastle Amateur Dramatic Society, after which it was "cleared for dancing" and chinese lanterns "glowed in the evening" - a tantalising image.

But there can be no doubt that the wooden pavilion is mentioned in an 1890 magazine published by Hansard London, called "Rainbow Sketch Book series No 1" the article is called "Axel Cooling in a Lincolnshire Spa" and states:

*"There is also a commodious building close to the tennis grounds, which is utilised for fetes, bazaars, garden parties, concerts, etc."*

Local people called it 'The Barn', and photographs prove the existence of tennis courts close to the Pavilion and also show cricket matches. Some years later it had acquired a verandah, and spectators are shown seated inside it. In 1895, a new nine-hole golf course was created with its first tee near the Pavilion, but by 1911 the course was gone, having been superseded by the great Hotchkin course which has made Woodhall Spa so famous in the golfing world. On the Ordnance Survey map of Woodhall Spa of 1905, the Pavilion and verandah are clearly marked. That same year, the Baroness von Eckhardstein was planning her country house, Petwood, in the woodland nearby. Divorcing the Baron, she then married Archibald Weigall, a grandson of the Eleventh Earl of Westmorland, in 1910.

The Weigalls lost no time helping to plan the great Pageant of 1911 which celebrated the Centenary of the discovery of the Spa waters. Much of this event took place in the Pleasure grounds next to the Pavilion. The Borough guide of 1911 mentions cricket matches and the fine ground "Possessing a comfortable pavilion under the delicious shade of some trees. Spectators at the most important fixtures have the pleasure of listening to the excellent band which ..... leaves the bandstand in the hotel grounds and plays close to the cricket pavilion."

Inside the Pavilion, parallel bars and dumb-bells were installed for the use of Spa and hotel guests and were used again by volunteers for the First World War to help them train. The remains of trenches which the volunteers dug can still be discovered in the north-east corner of the Petwood Estate.

Turnstiles, Laurel bushes and rustic huts girdled the Pleasure Grounds, and the Military Bandstand which had stood near the Victoria hotel and Spa Baths was transferred to a point west of the Pavilion. A rustic bandstand was built in the original position, and around the turn of the century the Tea House in the Woods opened, offering gifts and a lending library. The entire site was thus devoted to physical and mental refreshment, and the Pavilion was a multi-purpose sports and entertainment centre long before it became a cinema. When the Victoria hotel burned down at Easter 1920, the relationship between hotel and Pavilion was severed.

The rescuable furniture from this dreadful fire was stored inside the Pavilion, which could scarcely contain it all. After this, the concerts, plays and bazaars went on as usual. Then between August and October 1922, the Weigalls purchased the Victoria hotel ruins and land including the Pavilion, and the scene was set for a very optimistic announcement by Lady Weigall when she opened the Horncastle Ex Servicemen's Club:

> "Woodhall Spa is going to have the biggest boom it has ever had in its life".

That boom would depend largely upon the success of her cinema, to be housed 'temporarily' in the old wooden pavilion which had witnessed so much of Woodhall Spa's history. That the Kinema has survived and prospered in that same building to the present day would surely have amazed her.

# THE KINEMA IN THE WOODS

The original Pavilion c.1890 when it was known as The Barn and did not yet have its verandah. To the right, beyond The Barn, is the Spa Baths building, the Bandstand and the Victoria Hotel.

A superb close-up of the bowling and floral border in front of the pavilion in 1906.

The Spa Pleasure Grounds before 1920. Tennis is being played in the foreground and the Pavilion can be seen behind the Bandstand which had been moved from its original position by The Victoria Hotel.

THE KINEMA IN THE WOODS

The Pavilion Cinema in the early 1920's, with its original doors. A small vestibule can be detected.

The Pavilion cinema with Captain Allport's office to the left and an extended vestibule built out from the facade. Note the roof lights. Probably mid 1920s.

# THE KINEMA IN THE WOODS

View of the Kinema in late August 1931, after the name change of 1930. Lupino Lane in The Yellow Mask was on at the time and there is now a roof extension from both sides of the vestibule. The roof lights have gone, and raised ventilators have taken their place. Note also one of the flues from a coke stove.

From left to right may be seen the young Ron Webb, Freda Atkin, and possibly David Whyles, with Captain Allport seated. The car is a Humber.

THE KINEMA IN THE WOODS

The facade in late August 1931 with, next to Captain Allport's office, a chocolate machine and a weighing machine - an intriguing juxtaposition!

The unique setting of "THE KINEMA IN THE WOODS"
Amidst the health giving air of the Pine Woods

**SOUND ENTERTAINMENT.**

Clear and Distinct TALKIES,

Pleasant to the Ear.

Mondays, Tuesdays, Thursdays and Fridays at 7-45 p.m.

Wednesdays and Saturdays at 6 and 8 p.m.

*Telephone :* 66
*Woodhall Spa.*

A page from the 1931 booklet 'Woodhall Spa for Health & Sunshine', taken at the same time as the previous image.

An advertisement for Kinema Wireless equipment of the early '20s. Captain Allport fitted similar equipment in March 1925.

The deck chairs and curtains after the post - Second World War refurbishments. The curtains were dark blue velvet opera swags with shields in gold and a blue silk slash across. Note the antimacassars on the deck chairs!

# THE KINEMA IN THE WOODS

A view from further back, with cigarette stub marks on the back of the fixed seating, and 2s 6d marked on the post indicating the seat price difference.

The projection room showing No 1 and No 2 projectors with, top left, extractor chimney from arc lamp, and on right above No 2, the top spool box and mechanism. This was a Premier end of spool audible indicator, and the bell rang when the film reel was coming to an end.

# THE KINEMA IN THE WOODS

Over 5,000 Sold in the UNITED KINGDOM.

POWER'S No. 6
Puts the Picture on the Screen.
The **Walturda W** Co., 46 GERRARD St.
Regent 5310. Ltd., LONDON, W. 1.
Albertype, Westrand

An advertisement for a Powers No 6 projector similar to the original one used in the earliest days.

The projection room re-equipped in 1984 with the Kalee 21 projector and Westrex Tower and showing a British Acoustic header amplifier and Ferrograph tape recorder for incidental music.

# THE KINEMA IN THE WOODS

Lessee:
Capt. C. C. Allport,
"Sylvanhay,"
Woodhall Spa

Telephone:
2/66, Woodhall Spa

Station:
Woodhall Spa.,
L. & N.E. Railway

Telegrams:
2/66, Woodhall Spa

WOODHALL SPA,
LINCOLNSHIRE

1938

TERMS OF EMPLOYMENT.

The Management and Staff of the Kinema in The Woods hereby agree respectively to employ and be employed on the terms of the following statement.

The Management will pay the weekly wages mutually agreed subject to one week's notice on either side, and in the event of an employee being off work through sickness will continue his pay for two weeks. At the end of the two weeks employment and pay will cease unless and until the employee returns to work.

The Staff agree to work on Bank holidays and to put in any extra time when required, and to take on extra duties during holidays or sickness, without extra pay, during the first two weeks.

The Management agree to grant the Staff two weeks holiday with pay each year at a time suitable to the Management.

On behalf of the Management:-
C C Allport

On the part of the Staff :-

I agree to the above terms. (Signed) D.Whyles.

I agree to the above terms (Signed) R.G.Webb.

I agree to the above terms. (Signed) R.G.Croft.

Terms of employment for all concerned in 1938.

# Woodhall Spa Kinema
## MONTHLY GAZETTE

Edited by C. C. ALLPORT.

**MARCH, 1927.**

ENTER—The Enlarged GAZETTE.

*"Business without advertising is like winking at a girl in the dark."*
          Sir WALTER DE FRECE, M.P.

In presenting the first number of the enlarged Monthly Gazette, I take the liberty of quoting the above phrase, which seems to me to admirably fit the occasion; and I should like to take this, the first opportunity, of expressing my appreciation to all those business friends who have so readily given their support and made this venture possible. I feel certain that my Patrons will realise the value of this support, and that they will help to ensure the advertisers an ample reward for their enterprise.

Among the new features will be found a list of forthcoming attractions for a short period beyond the present month, and various paragraphs of news and general interest in connection with films, stars and other matters.

*C C Allport*

---

WILLIAM BOYD was asking the crowd in the studio the other day if they knew the difference between ammonia and pneumonia.

After a number of guesses they gave it up. "One comes in a bottle, the other in a chest," he explained with a smile.

THE first cinema in this country was opened at Islington by Mr. A. E. Chapman, in August, 1901.

Lord Burnham, the great newspaper proprietor, speaking at a meeting of the Faculty of Arts, deplored the snobbish attitude in regard to British films by important people at the head of large and authoritative bodies, and urged the breaking down of prejudice and the active co-operation of associations and clubs to place the cinema on as high a plane as any of the other arts, and to see that the prestige of British cinematography was recognised all over the world.

---

## COLLINS & CO.,
### :: :: The Old Established Chemists.

SELECTED DRUGS   ACCURATE DISPENSING.
:: PROMPT ATTENTION TO ALL ORDERS. ::

NEAR ST. PETER'S CHURCH AND KINEMA.   Phone 5.   **WOODHALL SPA.**

---

The Kinema's Monthly Gazette, front page, March 1927.
Captain Allport extols the virtues of the British film industry in his leading article.

## THE KINEMA IN THE WOODS

**THURS., 8th June, FRI. and SAT.**
Diana Churchill, Jean Muir,
Peter Murray Hill and Fred Emney in
**JANE STEPS OUT**
Everyone stepped on Jane—then Jane rebelled—so see what happens when "Jane Steps Out !"

— SPECIAL NOTICE —
The Projection room is being rebuilt and enlarged and at the same time central heating is being installed, and the Management regret that it will be impossible to complete this work without a temporary stoppage, and the Kinema will therefore be closed for two weeks from Monday, 12th June and will re-open on Monday 26th June. The Management hope that patrons will be extra attentive to the excellent films in this programme as some compensation for the closed period.

26th June.      Claude Hulbert in
"HIS LORDSHIP REGRETS"
29th June.      Charles Laughton in
"ST. MARTIN'S LANE"
3rd July.       In Technicolour
"The Adventures of ROBIN HOOD"

**MAY-JUNE - - - 1939**

# THE KINEMA IN THE WOODS

Tele. 2166.          WOODHALL SPA.

Mondays & Thursdays at 5 & 7-45.
Tuesdays & Fridays at 7-45 p.m. only
Wednesdays & Saturdays, 5-45 & 8.

Old Age Pensioners and Unemployed admitted at half-price.

**MON., 15th May, TUES. and WED.**
Fred Astaire, George Burns,
Gracie Allen, Joan Fontaine
and Reginald Gardner in
**A DAMSEL IN DISTRESS**
From one of the funniest stories by P. G. Wodehouse.

Front and back of the small folded card programme May - June 1939, announcing the rebuilding of the projection room etc. in mid-June.

Cinematograph Exhibitors Association Certificate of November 14th 1923.

# REEL 3
## A Very Shaky Start

*"Monday night was a big evening for Woodhall Spa. It saw the commencing of the boom promised by Sir A. and Lady Weigall, when the new cinema in the Pavilion was open and a long-felt need in the Spa was an accomplished fact".*

Horncastle News August 15th 1922.

Lady Weigall had arranged with Mr A. Vidler of the Grand Electric cinema in Lincoln for the latest films to be supplied, and had invited him to make a speech on the opening night, September 11th. No doubt with some embarrassment, Mr Vidler announced that the film **The Lion Eaters** had not arrived and that a Charlie Chaplin film would be shown instead. The exact film was not recorded, and to date, no one can remember what it was, but it could well have been **The Kid** with little Jacky Coogan.

Sir Archibald then introduced a film made during his Governorship of South Australia of the visit of the Prince of Wales to Adelaide, thereby reminding the audience of the Weigalls' royal connections. Earlier, he had expressed dismay at all the 'long faces' of the Spa residents on his return home, and a 'complete absence of cheery optimism.' Wondering how the residents could have 'let things slide', he said he was 'astonished they had survived at all'! The cinema was designed to counteract this gloomy tendency and to lift everyone's spirits. Furthermore, he hoped it would open on a Sunday night, for 'if people would not go to church, they must take the church to the people, and much good might be obtained from the right kind of film.' Thus, the Pavilion Cinema got off to a rather heavy-handed start!

The heavy hand of Sir Archibald continued the following week when there were matinees of Australian films. Full houses were reported in the evenings. The Horncastle News gave the public enthusiastic descriptions of what could be seen:

> "A new startling serial, **The Diamond Queen**, will be screened. It is the thrilling adventures of beautiful Eileen Sedgwick, the girl who knows no fear. A Sunshine Comedy **Wild Women and Tame Lions** is screamingly funny".

These early films always reached a climax and then stopped, 'to be continued next week'. With the heroine tied to the railway tracks and a train approaching, the management hoped that its audiences would return to witness the outcome. However, on February 23rd 1923, with the Weigalls in Biarritz, the press warned that 'unless the Pavilion Cinema is better patronised it is likely to be closed. It rests with the Spa people themselves whether they have pictures or not'. By June 9th this crisis had passed, with takings and expenses just about level and Lady Weigall agreeing to keep the cinema open.

Rudolph Valentino as **The Sheik** came riding to the rescue. 'The new super-film, The Sheik, is booked for August. It is the galloping chief of screen sensations.' Extra seats had to be installed and there were full houses, and on August 25th we find that C. S. Eaton-Evans, as land agent for Sir Archibald, had applied for a Woodhall Spa cinema licence for the next twelve months, in the Horncastle police court.

The licence was granted for six days out of seven, and Mr Eaton-Evans was asked whether he had ever shown films on a Sunday to which he replied 'No'. Obviously Sir Archibald's big idea about screening morally uplifting films each Sunday could not be realised. A separate licence would have to be issued every time a film was shown on a Sunday.

The films were shown on a hand-cranked Powers No 6 projector which may have been the one Lady Weigall brought with her from Australia, and a borrowed projector which took over when a change of reel was required. The projectionist from the start was David Whyles, a local electrician, who during the next twenty five years would train several others to thread, show and rewind the films.

= REEL THREE =

By September 8th 1923 the film serial **The Three Musketeers** had reached episode twelve — 'The Brand of Fleur de Lys.' It was reported to be the most popular attraction yet shown at what the papers now called the Woodhall Spa Cinema.

On November the 17th, the press again reported 'a remarkable drop in attendance at the cinema. The management are somewhat concerned as to the cause.' Clearly Rudolph Valentino would be needed again and we read that 'Cinema goers will be pleased to know that the famous and popular Rudolph Valentino will appear during Christmas week.'

During this period, the Victory cinema Horncastle was advertising in a more eye-catching way and had the impresario Percy W. Teed as its proprietor. The Woodhall Spa cinema needed a similar figure with whom audiences could identify, and the ideal man arose in an enterprising young member of the Petwood Estate Office, Captain Carleton Cole Allport.

# REEL 4
## Allport in Charge

For its first fifty years, the Kinema was in the hands of a man who had fallen for Woodhall Spa in his youth, so much so that he cycled there regularly from Sheffield. Carleton Cole Allport, known to family and friends as Noel in order to distinguish him from his father, who was also Carleton, was born in Millhouses, Sheffield, in 1893.

His parents ran the post office in Conisborough, famous for its Norman castle. Young Noel cycled even further than Woodhall Spa, beginning his working life as an assistant to the New York village grocer Mr Holmes. He remembered coming to live in Woodhall Spa in January 1911 and getting a job in Captain Weigall's Estate Office in the recently built Petwood House.

In August 1914 he joined the 6th Battalion of The Lincolnshire Regiment as a private but was made a lance corporal a fortnight later. Commissioned in January 1917 he served in Gallipoli, but was sent home with dysentery. By the end of the War he had attained the rank of Captain. He returned to the Petwood Estate Office.

Before the First World War, cinemas in England had been thick on the ground. By the end of 1914 there were almost 440 cinemas in the London area and perhaps 4000 across Britain. Many closed for good when projectionists were drafted, films became hard to obtain and an amusement tax took effect from May 1916. When the Weigalls enlisted Captain Allport's assistance with their own cinema, there were already cinemas in Horncastle, Boston, and Lincoln, but Woodhall Spa was out on a limb despite superb rail links with London. All the films arrived by rail to Woodhall Spa station, and were conveyed in a converted bath chair attached to a bicycle, to the cinema itself.

## REEL FOUR

A press announcement of July 26th 1924 mentions the words 'Kinema' and 'C. C. Allport' for the first time. This would no doubt signal the time when Captain Allport took over the running of the place, and in line with most other cinemas of the period, decided to adopt the word Kinema from the Greek word for 'motion'. He adapted the western side of the Pavilion down to the start of the old verandah as his new office, and representatives of the film distributors would call on him there.

All the windows were open, because most of the reps smoked, a habit Captain Allport hated. He felt no qualms about refusing all the films on offer if none suited him, even after lengthy interviews. The reps were always treated courteously and offered a hot drink, but many went away disappointed.

The Kinema was licenced by the Board of Trade and because its licence number was 68 it has been supposed that it was only the 68th kinema to re-open after The Great War, but this cannot be so. The Kinematograph Weekly of June 1922 states that more than 4000 kinemas were already in operation. No special significance can attach therefore to the number 68.

The Board of Trade insisted that 33.3% of all feature films, and 25% of all support films, had to be British. This was known as the 'quota' and you were fined at the year end if this was not met. The Kinema's books were taken to a Justice of the Peace or Notary (a Mrs Sandy did this for many years) and Captain Allport had to swear on her bible that his entries were truthful. They were also immaculately written. Half the pages were then sent off to The Board. It is therefore no wonder that Captain Allport favoured British films.

A man would come once a year to Woodhall Spa representing the advertising company Ben Roberts of Leeds. He visited all the local businesses, co-ordinated the slides on which their adverts were shown, and took an annual sum for the slide to be screened. Captain Allport had a contract with Pathe News Reels and London film distributors in Leeds. He knew exactly what he wanted for his Kinema and steered it successfully through several troubled periods. If his staff tried to do things their way rather than his, he prevailed – and his quiet voice and affable manner helped him. Once, a rewind boy put a record on which the Captain did not find suitable, and ordering him to bring it to his office he calmly said "I thought I told you not to play this record", and smashed it over his own knee, adding "I should have done that a long time ago". No more was said.

Maj. C.C. ALLPORT
KINEMA 1922-1973

THE KINEMA IN THE WOODS

That smouldering look..... a detail of a Kinematograph Weekly advert showing Valentino in Blood and Sand (1922). Inset is probably the film's presenter Jesse L. Lasky.

A Pavilion Kinema advert for the film which made Rudolph Valentino a star in 1921. The Zane Grey westerns were also very popular.

A Kinema advert of 1927, showing one of the many almost forgotten heroines of the silent screen, Estelle Brody.

> Entertainments, Etc.
>
> **Woodhall Spa Pavilion Kinema.**
> TELEPHONE: 66.
>
> TO-NIGHT (FRIDAY), Commencing at 7.45 p.m
> TO-MORROW (SATURDAY), at 6 and 8 p.m., Continuous.
> "HEIRS AND GRACES."
>
> MONDAY and TUESDAY NEXT, commencing at 7.45 p.m.
> WEDNESDAY at 6 and 8 p.m. Continuous.
>
> "MADEMOISELLE from ARMENTIERES"
> with ESTELLE BRODY
>
> Thursday, Friday and Saturday next week:
> "FORLORN RIVER."

The final scene of The Yellow Mask, 1931, in which Dorothy Seacombe, the heroine, rings down the curtain on Warwick Ward, the villain.

THE KINEMA IN THE WOODS

PICTURES FROM THE FILM    Page 32 KINEMATOGRAPH WEEKLY    February 23, 1939

## "TROUBLE BREWING"

It is forecast that the great reception given to George Formby's last film, "It's In The Air," will be repeated when A.B.F.D. Trade show the new Formby comedy, TROUBLE BREWING, at the Phoenix Theatre, Thursday, February 23rd, at 8.30 p.m. Produced by Jack Kitchin and directed by Anthony Kimmins, TROUBLE BREWING gives George the role of a lifetime, and he is supported by such excellent artistes as Googie Withers, Gus McNaughton, Garry Marsh, Martita Hunt, C. Denier Warren, etc.

George Formby's films were very popular at the Kinema and here he is seen with Googie Withers, Martita Hunt and others in Trouble Brewing of 1939.

A flyer for Brief Encounter (1945) with Celia Johnson and Trevor Howard.
*Courtesy of Carlton International Media Ltd - LFI.*

THE KINEMA IN THE WOODS

The Rank Organisation presents

GASBAGS

Rank Comedy Series

FROZEN LIMITS

OKAY FOR SOUND

ALF'S BUTTON AFLOAT

# THE CRAZY GANG

The Crazy Gang (Flanagan & Allen, Nervo & Knox, Naughton & Gold) made some very funny films in the '30s, with Alistair Sim as the Genie of the Button in Alf's Button Afloat.

*Courtesy of Carlton International Media Ltd - LFI.*

TO END A PERFECT DAY
(or improve an imperfect day!)
VISIT

# The Kinema in the Woods

Where every Film is Personally Selected for it's
ENTERTAINMENT VALUE.

---

Whit-Monday at 5.30 and 7.45 - Tuesday at 7.45
Wednesday at 5.30 and 7.45

ELEANOR POWELL - DENNIS O'KEEFE and our grand old veteran-SIR C. AUBREY SMITH in

## SENSATIONS of 1945 (U)

A Glorious Musical Comedy.

---

Thursday, 29 May at 5.30 and 7.45 - Friday at 7.45
Saturday at 5.30 and 7.45

MARLENE DIETRICH - JAMES STEWART in

## DESTRY RIDES AGAIN (A)

Return Engagement of the famous Western Comedy Drama

---

FREE CAR PARK and CYCLE SHELTER

A Kinema advert from the Official Opening of the Jubilee Park booklet, May 26th 1947.

# REEL 5
## Lured by Chocolates

The twenties were in the main a very lean and troubled time for Woodhall Spa and for the rest of the country. So many hopeful announcements were made about the rebuilding of the Victoria Hotel or salvation for the Spa Baths, only for hopes to be dashed. The Weigalls poured money into the Spa only to be criticised over the perceived dealings of their Agent and the doctors in the Spa Baths. Lady Weigall said she was deeply hurt and had thought of leaving Woodhall Spa which she said was so remote from London, until she remembered that she loved the place more than anywhere else.

She certainly helped the Kinema, by holding events there on many evenings when it would have otherwise been closed. Her friend Princess Marie Louise even attended illustrated talks there, one of which was 'The Garden of Allah' by a Rev. G. W. Kerr. For a time, in 1924, no advertisements were placed in the Horncastle News, and no films were previewed. But Captain Allport quickly made his mark as an enterprising business man, for in August the papers reported Kinema prizes of season tickets for three, two or one months, for his new competitions based on the films. In September 1925 he introduced a popular voting competition for the best films, and in October he announced that all children who attended the matinees of **Little Robinson Crusoe** with 'the most adorable boy on the screen', Jacky Coogan, would be given a bar of Jacky's favourite chocolate!

Lady Weigall and Princess Marie Louise regularly presented chocolates to any children who performed in song and dance shows in the Kinema. Miss Auckland's Cabaret Girls from Horncastle entertained at the Kinema on June 4th 1930 and were rewarded with boxes of chocolates. Once, Lady Weigall left behind a large box of Selfridges chocolates with her shawl, and Captain Allport decided that he and his staff ought to sample them. He was handing them round when her chauffeur appeared, to reclaim them. Perhaps Lady Weigall never noticed that several chocolates had disappeared.

Otherwise, the depressed times continued, with screenings down to two a week and attendances very poor throughout the winter of 1924-5. Things started to look up whenever Harold Lloyd or Buster Keaton featured, and in November: 25 **Rin Tin Tin** was very popular, to be followed on April 23rd 1926 with **The Wizard of Oz**, 'an attractive holiday picture'. This was of course the silent 1925 version.

The Captain tried everything to attract audiences, even installing wireless equipment in March 1925 so that patrons could have half an hour of 'listening in' prior to the films shown. This innovation had a startling result: The Horncastle News commented "That the installation is powerful enough is proved by the fact that it has been distinctly heard several hundred yards away from the Kinema".

One star the audiences never tired of was Rudolph Valentino, who was allowed out yet again as **The Sheik** in June 1927. Under a tenancy agreement of April 9th 1929, Captain Allport was confirmed as the tenant of the Kinema, paying an annual rent of £60. On July 6th of the same year, he addressed the public via the Horncastle News, on the subject of 'Talkies v. Silent Films.' His message is worth quoting extensively:

> *"Up to the present there are many I believe who feel that one of the beauties of the screen is its silence.... whether the wholesale introduction of talking films to the exclusion of silent films would be popular is at the moment very doubtful..... the Management of a London suburban Kinema, one of the first to install talkies, asked their patrons who overwhelmingly voted for a return of the silents ..... I am watching developments with considerable interest and shall be very careful not to make any change which I feel would be disappointing to lovers of the silent screen."*

Captain Allport was a good judge of the situation, for by October 1929 his Kinema was reported to be attracting large audiences, and Charlie Chaplin was featured in **The Gold Rush**, described as 'his greatest comedy'. 'Captain C. C. Allport maintains his high reputation for securing the best programmes', trumpeted the Horncastle News.

# REEL 6
## The Talkies Take Over

On September 6th 1930, Captain Allport announced the coming of the talkies. He had researched the best apparatus for showing the new 'talking' films and had opted for British equipment rather than American, travelling all over the country to many other cinemas. Characteristically, he was careful, saying that 'silent' fans need not despair because silent films would continue to be shown. His caution and reassurances paid off, for full houses rewarded his hard work, and one patron's views were used on a press advertisement: "better than anything I have heard in London. It's absolutely perfect." This must have been music to the Captain's ears, for he had yet again thought that this eighth season might have to be the last in the light of patchy attendances. He was ahead of Horncastle's Victory cinema, which did not announce its own talkies until November 1st, screening John Boles and Myrna Loy in **The Desert Song**. And he made a dramatic decision - from now on, the Kinema would be called The Kinema in the Woods.

Thus in the space of one week the Kinema we know today was born, and its first talkie was **Interviewing Wild Animals in Africa** by Major Ratcliffe Holmes, which was 'very heartily applauded'.

By October 18th the talkies were attracting huge audiences and an announcement was made to the effect that **Interference** would be 'the last silent film to be shown', giving an idea of the way the talkies swept all before them. But something had gone wrong between the Kinema office and the Horncastle News, because in fact, **Interference** was the first of Paramount's all-talkies, starring William Powell. It was a drama about a man who commits murder and turns himself in, in order to prevent his wife from being blackmailed, and Powell's voice was praised as much as his acting had been in the silent days. The Kinematograph Year Book uses 'FT' for 'full talkie', while some films were part-talkies (PT) with synchronised discs. The talkies also gave a new lease of life to the song, via the Musicals, and Woodhall Spa enjoyed the **Desert Song** in November 1930, and Al Jolson in **The Singing Fool** in December.

At this time Captain Allport was obtaining some films shortly after their release. One such was **The Yellow Mask**, starring Lupino Lane, which was released on May 11th 1931, appearing at the Kinema on August 22nd. Edgar Wallace's Mystery of Oriental villainy was followed in November by 'Sax Rohmer's great story', **The Return of Dr Fu Manchu**, a much more famous Oriental master criminal who inspired a long series of British two-reelers in the '20s, and several talkies, of which 'The Return' was one.

Screening the talkies had been a marvellous way to usher in the new decade, but the Weigalls were sad, for high taxes had forced them to relinquish Petwood House and they purchased their new home, Englemere at Ascot, in December. Petwood would eventually become an hotel with the Weigalls visiting frequently, but their golden age was almost over. They maintained control of some land in Woodhall including the Spa Baths, until a new figure appeared on Woodhall's stage, John Lewis.

# REEL 7
## Conflict and Resolution

The Kinema was for many years in privately owned grounds. The Spa Baths struggled to survive during the 'twenties and 'thirties, and were frequently closed in quieter periods of the year by the Spa Baths Trust under Sir Archibald Weigall. After John Lewis, an entrepreneur from Knightsbridge, took over in September 1930, he found Sir Archibald criticising him publicly for continuing to close the Baths, and a war of words ensued in the local press. However, Lewis also closed roads and pathways leading to the Baths and the Kinema for days on end, maintaining that his property was being destroyed or disfigured. There were many complaints from people who had been asked to pay to reach the Tea House and the Kinema. Colonel S. V. Hotchkin helped to persuade Lewis that at a time when the Woodhall Spa Advancement Association was doing its best to revive the town, Lewis might help by re-opening the Baths and the roads, and he did so on April 30th 1934. This is important because it highlights the problems Captain Allport had to deal with. Lewis was, from September 15th 1930, his new landlord, but deeds state that he did not own the actual contents of the Kinema. It is remembered in the town that Lewis disappeared at the beginning of 1935, selling the land back to the Weigalls in March, and leaving his wife behind at Rose Cottage! He had discovered that it was impossible to develop his part of the town as he had wished.

1935 saw the centenary of the building of the Spa Baths and ill-fated Victoria Hotel. The Weigalls reasserted their benevolent guardianship over The Baths and Kinema, and in April 1935 celebrated their only daughter Priscilla's twenty-first birthday by making her the sole owner of the Petwood Estate Company. Once again, Captain Allport was paying his rent to the Weigalls, and, as the new Chairman of the Woodhall Spa Urban District Council, he made a speech of thanks to Priscilla when on

April 25th she re-opened the Spa's Victoria Baths which she now owned. The Lincolnshire Standard proclaimed "Never has a more optimistic spirit prevailed in the Spa and district than at the present time".

Guests at the Kinema on Priscilla's birthday weekend may well have included Princess Marie Louise, Viscount and Viscountess Elibank, the Earl and Countess of Jersey, Viscount and Viscountess Scarsdale, and Lord Curzon who would soon become Priscilla's husband. This most brilliant few days in Woodhall Spa's history were brought to a climax on Saturday April 27th when Princess Marie Louise declared open the Royal Jubilee Grounds, the towns newest public amenity. In the evenings, the Kinema showed **The Thin Man** (1934) starring William Powell and Myrna Loy, and the following week there was an amateur dramatic production of Ivor Novello's Fresh Fields.

## A Steady Improvement

Captain Allport used his involvement with local politics to fight for the happiness of the community. He always greeted his Kinema customers and asked them what they thought of the films and what they would like to see in the future. And he took a fatherly interest in his staff, even opening bank accounts for them and visiting them when they were ill.

Fourteen year old Bob Croft joined the staff in 1937 and remembers Captain Allport's kindness. Once, as Bob was stoking one of the iron stoves, it exploded in his face as a result of a build-up of gas. In tears, he phoned the Captain, who calmed him down and left his home, Sylvanhay on Victoria Avenue, to go over and help him. Bob recalls that the old wooden walls of the Kinema, with their canvas sides towards the old verandah, had been rebuilt in brick, years before he arrived, and in 1939 a more solid brick-built projection room replaced the shed which had lasted for 17 years. The new projection room was built by A. F. Kirkby and Sons, the local builders, and featured fire-proof steel doors, a rewinding room, projection room, stoke-hole, generator, standby engine room and oil tank. The project closed the Kinema for a pre-announced fortnight in June, and a central heating system was installed at the same time. There would be no more exploding stoves!

Also in 1939, Captain Allport married Eva Bycroft, a local young lady who had helped him in the Kinema for years and who continued to do so until he died in 1973.

A deed of June 24th 1939 leased the Kinema to Captain Allport for twenty and three-quarter years at a yearly rent of £60 – the same rent he had paid all along.

THE KINEMA IN THE WOODS

The Kinema auditorium from the back row with the Compton organ up. The festoon curtains came from the Cinema at Towcester, Northants, when it closed in 1974. The ceiling house lights came from the Odeon, New Street, Birmingham.

The grey squirrel mural by Murray Hubick, painted on the east wall of the Kinema, is appropriately sited next to the woodland garden where there are many squirrels.

# THE KINEMA IN THE WOODS

Just inside the western door of the Kinema is Murray Hubick's mural of David Elliott as a commissionaire.

A river landscape by Nikolai Kukso. A mural painted shortly after the Second World War for the old vestibule. This one is by the west entrance to the kinema.

THE KINEMA IN THE WOODS

Bullrushes and water lilies painted by Nikolai Kukso just outside the east door to the Kinema.

THE KINEMA IN THE WOODS

A proud moment for Sheila Bycroft as Major Allport presents a watch to mark her first 25 years at the Kinema. April 1968.

Major Allport presides over Kinema Too, so called in order to assure patrons that the second auditorium is also a Kinema! Murray Hubick produced this quietly genial image from a photograph.

THE KINEMA IN THE WOODS

Kinema Too from the back row. The French pleat curtains came from the Regal Cinema Daventry in 1972, while the colourful house lights were originally installed in the Paramount Cinema, Manchester. Murray Hubick's murals adorn the walls and Major Allport gazes down from above the entrance.

The mural on the western wall of Kinema Too shows the Lincolnshire landscape seen through wide arches. View from the entrance door.

# THE KINEMA IN THE WOODS

Murray Hubick's Lincolnshire landscape seen from the rear of Kinema Too.

The Kalee 7 projector displayed in the foyer with an original poster of The Kid starring Charlie Chaplin and Jackie Coogan. The projector was able to be hand-cranked, and patrons were invited to turn the handle. (See projection appendix ii)

46

The pit which will house the Compton organ is dug beneath the demolished stage in the Kinema. Shawn Thomas, a projectionist, does the spade work while Cassie the dog looks on.

David Hill assembles the ranks of pipes for the Compton organ's pipe chambers.
See organ specifications, appendix i.

# THE KINEMA IN THE WOODS

## MEMORIES
### are made for this....
### JAMES GREEN at the GRAND PIANO

James Green, equally at home playing the piano or the Compton organ, seen here on a Kinema postcard.

*A feature of the "Down Memory Lane" shows at the Unique Kinema in the Woods are the piano and Compton Organ Duets*

Alan Underwood at the Kinema organ console. He literally grew up with the Compton Kinestra starting at the age of 13 and performing regularly for 10 years until 1998. He has now returned.

# REEL 8
## The Flicks in the Sticks

During the Second World War when for some of the time the now Major Allport and his wife were on the Isle of Man, the Kinema kept going. He felt very strongly that service men and women stationed at Woodhall Spa would need a boost to their morale, and somewhere to view the all-important reconnaissance films on days prior to bombing raids. By then, the Allports had started their family of three sons, and in one letter from the Isle of Man to their projectionist and friend Ron Webb, Eva requested baby clothes, while the Major advised Webb to inspect some new equipment in Horncastle before installing it at the Kinema. Eva returned to run the Kinema during her husband's absence.

Major Allport was now running a Camp for Internees on the Isle of Man, having previously overseen a similar camp near Leicester. Thanked by the Norwegian government for his excellent treatment of the Norwegian boys and officers, he received Crown Prince Olaf several times. Meanwhile the Kinema opened its doors and its 365 seats to the airmen, soldiers and WAAFs stationed at Woodhall and Coningsby.

They called it 'the flicks in the sticks' and the name became famous. Staff in the paybox remember the young service men and women queuing right round the Spa Baths or down Coronation Road. If the airmen booked seats for a matinee, it meant they would be flying on raids from R.A.F. Woodhall later that night. They came regularly in the week, but not on Saturdays when they would go to dances locally. Because the Kinema was hidden by dense woodland it became the ideal secret place to view rushes of film of low level flying raids and bomb-aiming practice, in preparation for dangerous raids like the ones the 'Dambusters' made on the Moehne, Eder and Sorpe dams in May 1943.

REEL EIGHT

A year later, with the officers of 617 squadron now installed at Petwood House, awaiting attacks on the Tirpitz and engaged in other daring raids, some relief from tension was afforded by a night out at the Kinema. Perhaps the airmen didn't know that the Kalee 8 projectors had been obtained from a bombed cinema in Leeds. They replaced two Kalee 7's, but the old carbon-arc lanterns were fitted onto the new Kalees because they were superior to those brought by the men from Leeds.

Ron Webb was the projectionist during the war and his wife Ellen (Nebby) worked in the paybox as did Millie Reader, Mrs Johnson and Mrs Allport. Lewis Johnson, who stoked the boilers, worked with Ron Webb and David Whyles in the projection box. Whyles, the Kinema's original projectionist, ran an electrical shop in Station Road, and Ron Webb learned the ropes from him, having been employed in the shop.

Whenever reconnaissance films were shown, the Kinema staff were sworn to secrecy. Many of the 'Arnhem boys' in their red berets (red for the Parachute Regiment) also saw films of the place where they would land on September 17th 1944 in a huge Allied campaign. Many never returned, for two Panzer Divisions were refitting in the Arnhem area and the boys fell upon them. Kinema staff recalled with sadness that so many were never seen again.

Pete Osborne began working in the Kinema as a 'spool boy' rewinding the spools of film in the early '40s. He remembered that he wasn't allowed to mind a projector for six months or do the changeovers. But the projection room was by no means a male preserve, for a seventeen year old girl called Sheila Bycroft (no relation to Major Allport's wife Eva) had been set on in April '43 as a rewind girl and she was followed by others. She remained for 37 years, developing a passion for films and becoming the Major's mainstay. David Whyles left the Kinema during the war to be an electrical engineer at R.A.F. Coningsby and R.A.F. Woodhall, as did Lewis Johnson.

What did the servicemen actually watch in the Kinema? Taking a small sample from 1944, they could enjoy, as the year progressed, **Old Mother Riley's Circus** with Authur Lucan, **Saboteur** with Robert Cummings, **You're In the Army Now** with Jimmy Durante, **Louisiana Purchase** with

Bob Hope, **They Died With Their Boots On** with Olivia De Havilland and Errol Flynn, **The Maltese Falcon** with Bogart, Mary Astor and Sydney Greenstreet, **In Which We Serve** with Noel Coward and John Mills, and **Citizen Kane** with Orson Wells. There were also several war films which threw the spotlight on various campaigns and which engendered pride and patriotism in the audiences of the time.

The seating in the Kinema in the mid '40s was very unusual. Major Allport bought a lot of red tip-up seats and put them directly behind the deckchairs, and behind these new seats were red plush 'loving couple' seats which had been there from the start. They were moved back and there were two forms at the rear, then the paybox immediately beyond a partition. After the servicemen had gone, the Major decided to have a refurbishment. Millie Reader's father Ted, and Stan Oakey, a local plasterer, did all the rounded corners of the pillars in the auditorium which we still see today. Sleight and Crookes, the painters and decorators from Woodhall Spa were brought in to put all the foundation colours onto the walls and Mr Crookes sometimes worked in the paybox while his wife was an usherette who also looked after the ice creams and sweets.

The marbling effect and the two pastoral scenes to the left and right as you enter the auditorium were painted by Nikolai Kukso, a talented artist who was one of many Polish soldiers living in Woodhall just after the war. He had a studio in the outbuildings of Halstead Hall near Stixwould and he painted three ceilings in Martin Hall representing Spring, Summer, and Autumn, and a Madonna and Child for The Roman Catholic Church in Woodhall Spa. The lighting was changed, and increased; cream shades were put on tungsten lamps and there was a 'silence please' light box which the Major would switch on if the audience at the rear were noisy! Wally Cooper, an Australian who had flown Lancasters, used his vast knowledge of electronics to build the carbon arc rectifier, and a new single channel sound system which was duplicated in order to allow for valve failure.

Major Allport had excellent hearing, and would instruct over the inter-com about the level of volume he required. On one occasion he told Mr Whyles the volume was too low and needed putting up half a point on the resistance-slide control. Whyles was indignant and shot the

## REEL EIGHT

volume right up, bringing it back to where he'd had it originally. The Major phoned again, knowing it was not set as he had wished, and ordered Whyles to do it properly. Staff at the Kinema have always 'pitched in' and performed a variety of tasks, and it is to be expected that on some occasions Major Allport's orders would not go down too well. Sheila Bycroft often stomped off on such occasions but the Major's kindness always won her round. Bob Croft recalls that when his boss was given his new rank, he said "now that I have been made a Major, I shall be giving you a rise in wages". And when the inquisitive Pete Osborne asked him what he had done during his war service he modestly replied that he had been "in charge of internees", and left it at that.

# REEL 9
## Allport Soldiers On

The 1950's and 60's saw many improvements inside the Kinema but Major Allport also had to cope with dwindling audiences thanks to the rise of television. His adverts stressed how warm and comfortable the Kinema was, but he admitted to the local press that he was disappointed about the poor turnout, often showing films to only twenty people. He became grateful to people from a wider area who supported the Kinema regularly when the people of Woodhall itself did not. He and his wife delivered publicity leaflets to many villages surrounding Woodhall, and Eva recalls that she learned to drive on the back lanes, which were even quieter then than they are now. And if anyone along the way was kind enough to display a Kinema poster, they were given a half-price pass to the Kinema. But Major Allport always regarded the Kinema as his hobby, and he usually made a slight loss. Three times chairman of Woodhall's Urban District Council, he threw himself into campaigning and got a petition up to keep Kirkstead Bridge free of tolls. It succeeded.

The Major was also enthusiastic about a nation-wide road safety competition for children, sponsored by Outspan, and always accompanied the four local girls and their supporters in the coach whenever they competed in quizzes. Jean Robinson (now Stollery) was the fourteen year old captain and she remembers them winning through to the semi final, whereupon Major Allport gave them one month's free Kinema visits as 'a very nice reward for our efforts.' This was in May 1958.

On November 24th 1950 Lady Weigall died, and was followed on June 3rd 1952 by Sir Archibald. One of his final acts was to convey 'The

Kinema in the Woods with lands adjoining comprising 3962 square yards, to Carleton Cole Allport in fee simple …. of £1060.' The deed is dated January 23rd 1952. Thus for his last 21 years there, Major Allport was the owner.

One of his decisions in his new role was rather agonising, for with new regulations about seating having to be fixed to the floor, he realised that the deck chairs would have to go. In a way, they symbolised the Weigalls and the old cricket pavilion, and all had now gone. He said he had pondered various ways they might be attached to the floor but had decided it was not possible. Their demise does not seem to have been noted in the local press, and Sheila Bycroft said she thought they went in 1953 but others think they remember them being there some time later. A detailed press article of 1973 states that the deck chairs went in 1957.

## The Major Says **NO**

Two long boxes of index cards supplied by the distributors, describing films in detail, were found in the Kinema. Annotated by Major Allport, they give a vivid idea of the pivotal role he played before films actually reached the Kinema's screen. The key printed on the cards themselves was amusing enough:

> 'films marked thus (symbol) are suitable chiefly for good class houses. marked thus (symbol) are suitable chiefly for popular houses.'

But Major Allport was not unduly swayed by the critical remarks on these cards whether they were praising or damning the films; he put **NO** in pencil on a majority of them, and VG or FG for very or fairly good. **Girls in Prison** (1956), A 'heavy prison drama with religious undertones …. some of prison scenes are distasteful', merited **NO!**, while **Hot Rod Girl** (1956) 'built on the proposed banning of hot-rodding (driving old unworthy cars at speed on a special track) in a small town', received a very firm **NO**. Even Hitchcock's **The Lady Vanishes** got a **NO**, but could have been screened before, since some cards described re-issued films.

**The Blue Lamp** (1950) with Dirk Bogarde and Jack Warner earned a G from Major Allport, as did **The Baby and the Battleship**, 1956, starring John Mills, Richard Attenborough and Bryan Forbes. The Major said **NO** to Vivien Leigh's **Anna Karenina** (1948) but a big **YES** to **The Wicked Lady** (1949) with Margaret Lockwood and James Mason. He was perhaps nonplussed by a Powell and Pressburger film **Black Narcissus** (1947) described as 'First rate entertainment for discriminating people', rating it only 'fairly good'. But he always favoured family films about animals, and **Brumas Steals the Show**, 1950, about London Zoo's famous Polar bear cub, got a G. Finally in this brief sampling **Confession** (1955) with Sydney Chaplin, Audrey Dalton and John Bentley, described as 'not a nice picture' was stabbed with a large firm **NO** and underlined in pencil.

How did people in surrounding villages reach the Kinema in the fifties, when few owned a car? The answer was the cinema bus or 'buzz', which went out on a Saturday evening. Saturday night was 'pictures night' with fish and chips afterwards, then the return home. Milson's, and Goslings of Mareham ran special bus services, with their cream and maroon or cream and green coaches.

1957 was a big year for the Kinema, with **Reach For the Sky** being screened in January for an entire week. At that time, it was virtually unheard of for films to be screened any longer than two or three days, but **Reach For the Sky** had been a box-office sensation, telling the story of indomitable war hero Douglas Bader, played by Kenneth More. On only one previous occasion had Major Allport screened a film for a whole week, showing the Queen's Coronation in colour in 1953.

By late February '57, a new wide screen had been installed. Made in America, it was seamless, and the roof had to be raised to accommodate it. In July came new Cinemascope equipment, identical with that at the Empire, Leicester Square. The first film shown through the new Cinemascope lenses was **The Eddie Duchin Story** with Tyrone Power and Kim Novak, followed by **The King and I**, and **Carousel**.

For his last decade, Major Allport had the help of another female full time employee who joined Sheila Bycroft in the projection room. Her name was Amy Dulake and she started work on September 3rd 1963. Amy came to the 'front of house' in the 1980's as manager. Both ladies featured in 'women's lib' style press articles, and were joined for twenty years by Amy's mother Beatrice who volunteered as a cleaner and only left when she was eighty in 1995. She was to take on a most important role in the years following the Allport era, as will be seen. Towards the end of his fifty years at the Kinema, Major Allport saw bigger audiences return. Interviewed by the Lincolnshire Standard on April 28th 1972 he said that the last two years had been ' the best ever, and people come here from miles around.' They did indeed, and one couple used to come regularly from Grimsby, for a very long time.

When the Major renewed the Kinema licence for the fiftieth time, he was given it free of charge – a recognition of extraordinary achievement. He died in July 1973 at the age of 80, and of course he made the front page of the Horncastle News.

In the Lincolnshire Echo of August 8th 1973 Mrs Allport announced the sale of the Kinema to 'a cinema owner from Daventry', and said 'the film industry is becoming more and more complicated and it is a difficult job ordering films and obtaining new releases. The present staff will be kept on.'

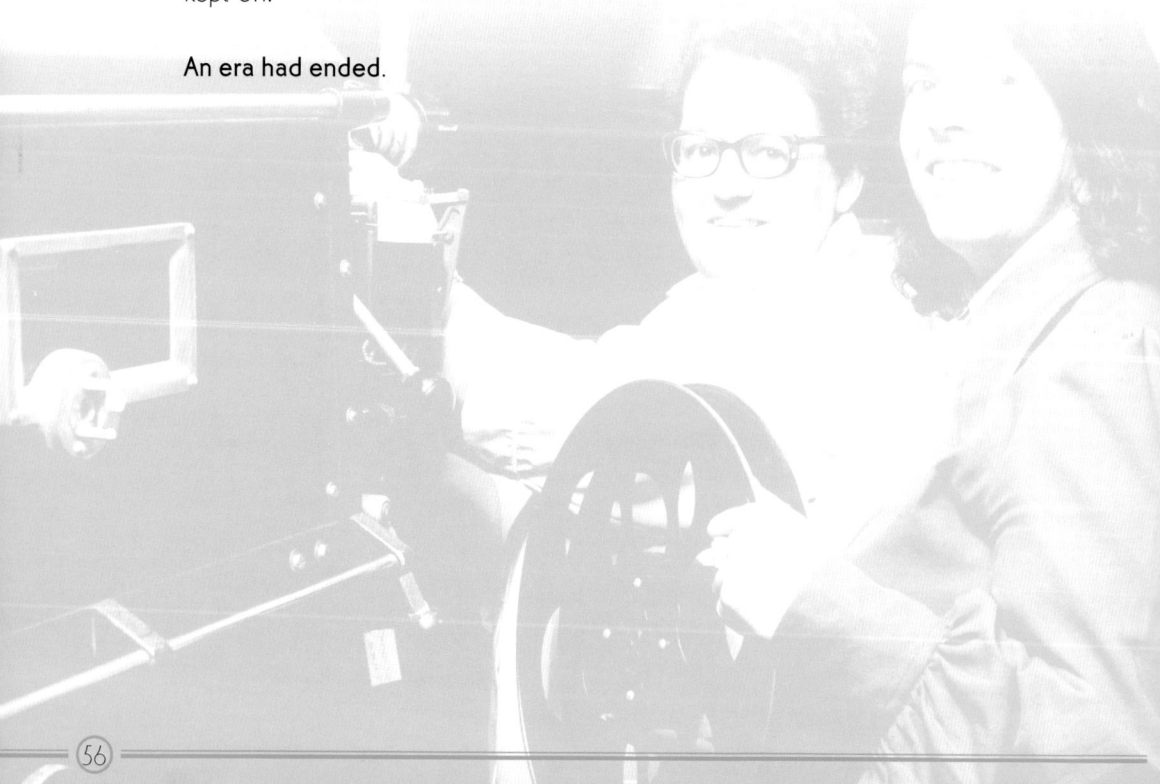

**An era had ended.**

# REEL 10
## New Era, New Facilities

The 'man from Daventry' was James Green, himself a rewind boy at the age of fourteen when, at the town's Regal cinema, he started work for 7s 6d a night. That was in 1963, and eventually he became the chief projectionist.

In 1971 he took a lease on an old cinema at Stone in Staffordshire, and got it back on its feet. Enthusiastic about old cinemas, their organs and their music, he came over to see the Kinema in 1973, meeting Major Allport twice just before he died, and decided to take the place on. He needed all his youthful energy, for two years later he bought the derelict Franklin cinema at Spilsby, renaming it the Phoenix, and then, when the lease ran out on the Picture House at Stone in 1978, he decided to re-use all the Art Deco fixtures and fittings for his new Bijou cinema at Mablethorpe, which was built on the site of a demolished amusement arcade, in 1981.

At that time, having three cinemas came in handy, for they gave him the booking power to obtain recent releases far sooner than Major Allport had been able to do.

James Green opened at the Kinema on Monday August 6th 1973 with **Clockwork Orange**, a notorious film which film critic Dilys Powell labelled 'the most audacious of horror films. And the most inhuman.' Not that the film told Woodhall Spa anything much about its new Kinema owner, whose favourite film is the 1948 black and white **While I Live** with Sonia Dresdell and Tom Walls. Decimalization had arrived, and patrons now paid 45p for any seat in the house. Twelve years later, a seat would cost only £2 with children at £1. James told the press that he wanted people to feel they could easily afford a night out at his cinemas. Like his predecessor, he put the comfort of his patrons first, and reduced

# REEL TEN

the number of seats from 365 to around 320, retaining some large green Dunlopillo seats supplied by Walturdaws. At this time, in 1974, a raised floor was introduced, rising to the rear of the auditorium, and enabling people seated further back to get a better view of the screen. At the same time, a foyer was created, remedying an omission which had now become a necessity.

Two Kalee 12 projectors were installed in 1978, which although electronically controlled, relied on the traditional carbon arc lamps. Today, Xenon bulbs are used. David Hill, a young organ builder from Caistor, was the part time projectionist at this time, starting in 1979 and leaving in May 1990.

Cyril Limb, (the Alford builder) provided many extra facilities for the Kinema in two phases, beginning in 1989. The additions meant that the new facade would be brought forward thirty feet — a considerable change.

County council guidelines on the preservation of historic buildings were taken into account for all phases of construction, which included a new office, ladies toilets and toilets for the disabled in 1989, and an extended foyer, new gents toilets, ante-rooms and Kinema Too, in 1994. Public consternation surfaced even before building work began, with people fearing the additions might be out of character, and they were especially anxious about Kinema Too, but the half-timbered style and matching gables, coupled with the fact that the facade did not seem to change much, soon calmed such fears. Planning permission, too, was a big worry and proved difficult to obtain, but the additions were needed if audiences were to be attracted back to the Kinema and away from their home videos. Meanwhile, some new means of generating income to help pay for the new work needed to be found. It came in the form of the Compton Kinestra organ.

\* \* \* \* \* \* \* \*

In 1986 James Green came across a most unusual survivor from the early days of kinemas when he visited Nigel Turner's nurseries at Harpole near Northampton. There, in one of the barns, was a red and gold lacquered Compton Kinestra organ console with all its pipes. It had come from Montague Pike's last cinema, the Cambridge Circus Cinematograph Theatre, which was restored after a fire and re-named the Super Cinema. The organ was originally installed there in 1927 or 8, and the renowned resident organist Edgar Peto designed the specification and gave the inaugural performance.

Made by John Compton, and specifically designed for use in the Kinemas of the day as a veritable Kinema Orchestra or Kinestra, it had an ornate console decorated in the eighteenth century Oriental style by a Japanese artist working at the London school of art. He moulded shapes of figures, animals and flowers in layers of gesso, then decorated them with applied gold leaf. It is known that he did two others, in white & gold and black & gold, but these have not survived.

In 1931 the SuperCinema was re-named the Tatler, and with sound films now being shown, the organ could have been neglected. The London organ builders Monk and Gunther removed the organ after the cinema frontage had been bombed, during a period when many cinema organs were broken up. Nigel Turner purchased the Compton in 1978 and added a third manual keyboard, a phantom piano and a Christie solid-state relay and capture system, making it unique amongst cinema organs.

The Compton Kinestra seemed ideal for the Kinema, and James Green purchased it from Nigel Turner. Earlier, he had played an electronic WurliTzer, installed at the side of the stage, but the Compton with its opulence, its history, and its sound coming from real pipes, would suit the Kinema down to the ground. First of all, however, it was necessary to go some way beneath that ground.....

In order to have the organ rise through the floor in the time-honoured manner, a pit would have to be dug at the front of the stage. The work began in November 1986 but Woodhall Spa's high water table proved to be a problem, with water from a spring trickling in at a depth of only 2ft 9ins or so into the soil. The digging would need to go to eleven feet, and a watertight capsule created using thick polythene liner, concrete and brick. The wood from the old orchestra pit was used to shutter the sides. Hugh Croft, the brother of former rewind boy Bob, was asked to advise on capping the spring and sucking the water out by hosepipe. He recommended a de-watering plant from Boston Divers, who were phoned promptly by Amy Dulake. Amy was part of the digging team which included James Green, Shawn Thomas, another projectionist, and Kinema gardener Bill Jesney. Indeed, James did the brickwork, and found it a deeply satisfying experience. By March 1987 the pit was finished and a painted steel lift was installed to carry the console. This had come from the Odeon (Regent) at Hanley which had a WurliTzer organ that had been removed. The lift was dismantled and brought to Woodhall in October 1986.

Two pipe chambers, one each side of the screen, were constructed to house the many pipes which David Hill would painstakingly assemble. Facing the audience, there appeared two sets of swell shutters which control the volume. The console was finally put onto the lift on April 12th 1987, and on October 29th at 7.30pm, the resident organist from Turners Musical Merry-Go-Round, young Nicholas Martin, rose through the floor playing the Compton Kinestra, and opened another new era in the Kinema's history.

## The Memory Lane Shows

The new organ played a starring role in the 'Down Memory Lane' shows which James Green presented on the last Sunday afternoon each month. They began in 1988 after James formed an alliance with the Tea House in the Wood. As he said to the Target on April 27th 1989, "tourists are not prepared to come here for a two hour film, but they will come in for a bit of everything". He played a medley of old favourites and audiences were invited to sing along to words appearing on the screen. Old Pathe news reels and other black and white film clips were shown, including footage of the Lancaster bombers, the funeral of King George V, the wedding of the present Queen, or even the great violinist Alfredo Campoli in a periwig and silk coat playing in a spectacular eighteenth century tableau, with dizzying multiple images. In August 1992, at a show commemorating the seventieth anniversary of the Kinema, James Green was thanked by David Radford of the Woodhall Spa Cottage Museum for preserving so much of Woodhall's history on the walls of the foyer, and some 300 people were taken on a tour which included the projection room. On this occasion a young man called Alan Underwood played the organ.

Alan Underwood's grandfather paid for him to have an hour on the Compton Kinestra in 1988 when he was only thirteen. Encouraged by James Green, he learned quickly and at fourteen was playing in his first Memory Lane Shows which required an hour off school in the afternoons. He played every weekend until 1998, and did duets (with James on the piano) of such favourites as 'The Dream of Olwen', and Ketelby's beautiful 'Phantom Melody'. Naturally, in order to accompany aviation films with aerobatics displays, he had to play 'Those Magnificent Men in Their Flying Machines' and The Dambusters March, and always finished the shows with 'I Do Like to be Beside the Seaside' because of its association with the great Reginald Dixon.

Sometimes a coach load of people from Nottingham would be in the audience, so Alan played Nottingham organist Jack Helyer's signature tune, 'I'm Happy When I'm Hiking' and said it always brought the audience to life! In the foyer, Alan enabled James to display a superb collection of old postcards of Woodhall Spa in its heyday, having collected them while learning the ropes of the family antique business. Together with old projection equipment, cinema posters and other memorabilia, they transform the foyer into a fascinating museum which adds to the Kinema's uniqueness.

James Green has always been a 'hands on' owner of all his cinemas, doing all those jobs which in the past Major Allport would have delegated to others. Amy Dulake has been a splendid assistant, and while she and James were refurbishing the cinema at Spilsby and helping to run it, her mother Beatrice virtually ran the Kinema between 1975-84, continuing the tradition of several members of a family pitching in to keep things running smoothly.

As for the continual seepage of water from that spring in the organ pit, an automatic electric pump today does the job of the original bucket and hosepipe, and so far no audiences have needed to flee in terror!

# THE KINEMA IN THE WOODS

TORFRIDA  Episode 3
Mrs. Archibald Weigall

HEREWARD THE WAKE  Episode 3
Capt. Archibald Weigall, M.P.

Two 1911 postcards from the Woodhall Spa Pageant showing the then Mrs Weigall as Torfrida, and Captain Archibald Weigall as Hereward the Wake.

Seen in this group photograph at Petwood in April 1935, Lady Grace Weigall in a huge fur collar is sitting next to her friend Princess Marie Louise, whose hat sports a white floral cockade. Seated below them is Lady Weigall's daughter Priscilla, wearing a dark scarf, while Sir Archibald Weigall sits to the left of the Princess. Lady Weigall founded the Pavilion Cinema in September 1922.

THE KINEMA IN THE WOODS

A Lincolnshire Echo photograph of the Kinema staff in the late 1940s.
L. to R.: Ron Webb (chief projectionist), Sheila Bycroft (second projectionist), Major Allport, Mildred Reader (now Matthews) (rewind girl) and Wally Cooper (Electrician).

Nikolai Kukso, painter of the foyer murals in the late 40s. The painting of King David playing his harp is now in the Morning Chapel in Lincoln Cathedral and was probably one of the items he restored there.

THE KINEMA IN THE WOODS

Sheila Bycroft being interviewed by Brian Johnston for 'Down Your Way' on June 20th 1976.

Sheila Bycroft and Amy Dulake in the projection room 1973.

Mrs Beatrice Dulake, who volunteered as a cleaner and ended up running the Kinema between 1975 - 84 seen here with her daughter.

Celebrating the Diamond Jubilee of the Kinema are Beatrice and Amy Dulake, and David Elliott, wearing Carl Coupland's commissionaire outfit.
Sunday August 29th 1982.

*Photo: Lincolnshire Echo*

# THE KINEMA IN THE WOODS

David Elliott's photograph of the 'Herbie Goes Bananas' vehicles outside the Kinema. These were loaned by the Walt Disney Company in celebration of the Diamond Jubilee of the Kinema, August 29th 1982.

Nicholas Martin coming up through the floor watched by a packed house as he inaugurates the Compton Kinestra organ in the Kinema on October 29th 1987.

*Photo: Horncastle News*

Hannah Hauxwell at the Compton organ in 1996. She became famous as a result of Yorkshire Television's film 'Too Long A Winter' when her lonely life of rural hardship touched many hearts.

The Unveiling of the plaque marking 100 years of British Cinema, on Sunday August 25th 1996. L. to R.: Darren Archer (projectionist), Alan Underwood, Lyn Needham (sweet counter), David Stephenson (usher), Joyce Stephenson & Brenda Robinson (sweet counter), Beatrice Dulake, Janet & James Green and their children, Mrs Eva Allport, Joy Swain, Amy Dulake, Derek Archer and Bob Croft.

*Photo: Horncastle News*

# THE KINEMA IN THE WOODS

Mrs Allport steps back to admire the B.F.I. plaque she has just unveiled, applauded by James Green.

Hugh Croft, consultant on the organ pit, with Cyril Limb the builder of Kinema Too, at the 75th birthday celebrations in September 1997.
Cyril Limb points to the early photographs of Petwood House, part of the Kinema's unrivalled display of images of old Woodhall Spa.

*Photo: Horncastle News*

The cutting of the cake on the 75th birthday celebrations, with from L. to R.: Amy Dulake, Janet & James Green, and Mrs Eva Allport.

*Photo: Horncastle News*

The Riley R.M. Nottingham Division Road Run of 1999 parks up for a Memory Lane Show!

## THE KINEMA IN THE WOODS

Film director Bryan Forbes with James Green outside the Kinema in late October 1999.

*Photo: Horncastle News*

Bryan Forbes' wife, actress Nanette Newman, seen outside the Kinema with young reporter Rowena Witham, late October 1999.

*Photo: Horncastle News*

# REEL 11
## Kinema Too and Future Plans

On Friday July 8th 1994, a second Kinema opened to the left of the new foyer, and screened the hit film **Four Weddings and a Funeral**. In any other modern multi-screen cinema, such places are merely curtained rooms, but Kinema Too can only be described as opulent, with its French pleats, festooned curtains, multicoloured and multi-layered house lights, and large murals by a Canadian artist, Murray Hubick. A grand piano and the Kinema's own design of carpet completed the 92 seat auditorium which was a response to modern demands by film companies that films be screened for more than a week. Having a second Kinema increases the choice which today's customers like to have.

The new murals were first displayed to the public in an artist's impression exhibited in the foyer. The impression was of course useful evidence when finance was being arranged for the project. Some people were hoping for more of the marble effect which makes the main auditorium so distinctive, but James Green had decided to create a new talking-point. He wanted to preserve the uniqueness of the original auditorium and to give Kinema Too its own special personality.

There is a splendid tradition of mural painting in Canada, ranging from those for the Canadian Pacific Railway to the mural town of Chemainus on Vancouver Island. Murray Hubick has created a new outpost for this tradition in Kinema Too. His brother's dog looks out from a window opening, painted in the 'trompe l'oeil' or 'fool the eye' manner. Major Allport looks out over the entrance door and there are leafy tendrils everywhere on the large mural of the Lincolnshire countryside on the opposite wall. Architectural fantasy in the stonework arches, painted by a scene painter from the Lincoln Theatre Royal, gives way to reality as a Lancaster bomber is seen in the sky, and Lincoln Cathedral is glimpsed on the horizon. With the birds, dog and plane, sounds are evoked in these murals as well as sights, and billowing gauzy draperies suggest the Lincolnshire winds!

Murray Hubick did not stop at Kinema Too, for just inside the two entrances to the main auditorium he painted a commissionaire, a squirrel, and other trompe l'oeil surprises. The commissionaire is a portrait of David Elliott who occasionally dons the uniform once worn by the cheeky Carl Coupland in the '50s. These murals complement the earlier ones in the foyer by Nikolai Kukso.

Although the entire spectrum of films is shown in Kinema Too, its intimacy lends itself to period pieces such as **Tea With Mussolini** or **Gosford Park**. Films are projected from the back of the tiered seating, in the conventional manner.

## Accolades and Anniversaries

The first Kinema anniversary to be celebrated by James Green was the 60th, in 1982, when the children's hit film **Herbie Goes Bananas** provided the theme. Walt Disney Productions provided the Herbie car (a miniature motorised Volkswagen) and a big banana full of children was towed along behind it.

The seventieth anniversary has already been noted, then on Sunday August 25th 1996, the Kinema's unique place in the history of the British Cinema was recognised with a commemorative plaque from the British Film Institute in the industry's Centenary year. One hundred cinemas throughout the U.K. had been chosen to receive a plaque, and it was placed on the external wall of Kinema Too and unveiled by Mrs Eva Allport. A number of former and current employees were present, but sadly Sheila Bycroft and Lewis Johnson had recently died. James Green paid tribute to them, and Mrs Allport congratulated him on the numerous improvements he had made to the building. Those assembled in front of the Kinema were told by James that the Kinema was now the only surviving one in the country to use rear projection and had been continuously operating since 1922.

The film director Bryan Forbes and his actress wife Nanette Newman visited the Kinema in October 1999. Bryan had spent some of his childhood in Woodhall Spa and wanted to feature the Kinema in his Radio 4 series about the history of the British cinema. He produced an atmospheric programme called 'The Flicks in The Sticks', broadcast on

January 25th 2000. James Green and Nicholas Martin were amongst those interviewed, and Mr Forbes recalled that whenever heavy rain bounced off the corrugated roof it would drown out the dialogue on the early talkies. The programme underlined the fact that the Kinema was a unique survivor, and enhanced its legendary status.

## Thoughts for the future

Since cinema began, the professional size of 35mm has been used to convey images to the screen, and from 1929 onwards this film also carried the synchronised soundtrack to go with the picture. It is inevitable that instead of thousands of feet of film showing at each performance, movies will be projected from a CD. or downloaded from the Internet onto special equipment and shown in the cinema environment. Film sound had been mono until the early '70s when stereo sound came into cinemas, and the Kinema and Kinema Too are both equipped with Dolby 5 channel Surround Sound. As with all the new technology coming along, James Green will be watching developments with much interest.

In 1999 planning permission was eventually granted for the building of a third Kinema which from the outside will be a mirror image of Kinema Too to make the facade more symmetrical. The proposed name of the new auditorium is 'Kinema Royal', named after the Royal Hotel which once stood at Woodhall's crossroads. The hotel was destroyed in the Second World War.

Since acquiring the Kinema 29 years ago James Green has carefully planned and executed many modernisations and upgradings to the facilities to enhance the enjoyment of his patrons. He has avoided dividing and sub-dividing the original building, preferring in many cases to take the harder route by sympathetically adding to the original construction.

Knowing the Kinema is so special, James sees himself as its custodian and is determined to keep and preserve this unique building so that it may be enjoyed for many years to come as a traditional British cinema, for as it says on the posters 'the Kinema in the Woods – there's nowhere quite like it'.

*And now it is time to go down memory lane....*

# REEL 12
## Down Memory Lane

The most vivid memory of the Kinema to appear in print was penned by the late Bill Skelton, a popular local journalist, in the Lincolnshire Standard of September 3rd 1982:

"In the earliest days it still had the trappings of a cricket pavilion. On hot summer days, the proprietor, Captain, later Major, Allport, would open up the sides a little."

"I went with my mother and father to see the silent films. Mrs Phillipa Tyler and Mrs Janet Enderby rattled the piano keys into a fury as the villain closed in on the heroine, or as the steam locomotive bore down on Pearl White chained to the rail track."

"The gentle tickle of the ivory keys as the lovers, who always won in the end, strolled off into the sunset, or somewhere. The build-up and then the dead silence as the villain crept up behind the hero to knife him in the back, and the anti-climax, not to mention irritation, as some wag in the audience would whisper loud enough to be heard all over the Kinema: "Behind you mate".

"Then came the talkies. The first I remember was **Ben Hur**, ..... in those days Christ was not seen on the screen. But I recall vividly his hand being shown. I can nearly smell the scene of the chariot race - it was oh so thrilling."

"Then came **Cape To Cairo**, **Sanders of the River**, featuring Paul Robeson, who I had heard singing in the Show Boat at Drury Lane the previous year. As I grew up in the thirties, there came the **Broadway Melodies**, Ginger Rogers and Fred Astaire and the magnificent sets; the cowboy films in which men were men and women were glad about that."

For many years, the bar of the ruined Victoria Hotel was still functioning and Kinema patrons could get a drink before the show. Sometimes the younger patrons entered in a rather merry condition, and on one occasion, having enjoyed a glass or two, two young men and their lady friend found their deck chairs at the front, whereupon the young lady went right through the ripped fabric, ending up with her legs in the air. Of course all three were helpless with laughter, and she couldn't do anything to right herself until her friends rescued her. At such moments Captain Allport would dim the lights to draw attention away from the commotion, and the trio skulked quietly away!

For the record, the original prices were three pence for the forms at the back, sixpence for seats next to the forms, nine pence for those next to the deck chairs, and one shilling for the deck chairs. But not everybody paid, and Mr and Mrs Hodson recall telling the commissionaire, Carl Coupland, that they had just come back from their honeymoon when he said, "Then you go in free!" This was in 1951, when nothing was free, and the couple were delighted. Major Allport's generosity has been noted, and so has Lady Weigall's, whose special Christmas shows with gifts brought by father Christmas, were gratefully remembered. Members of the Croft family often walked from Reeds Beck farm for a night out at the Kinema and particularly remember seeing **Little Lord Fauntleroy** in 1936, as a birthday treat.

Sheila Bycroft retired in 1980 after 37 years at the Kinema and said that if she'd had a £5 note for every time she'd shown **The Dambusters** film, she'd be a rich lady! She recalled that the Elvis Presley films were hugely popular and that the first Rock 'n Roll film she showed was **Rock Around the Clock** (1956) with Bill Haley and the Comets and Little Richard.

For the majority of patrons the Kinema was and is the passport to excitement, romance, and nostalgia. Long before the Compton organ appeared, a whole range of feelings was expressed through music, beginning with the phantom orchestra of piano, drums and cymbals, then from the large Panatrope discs which were synchronised with the silent films and played through Gyrotone equipment supplied by E. & N. F. French of Tamworth Staffordshire. These discs were played from the middle to the outer edge. Bob Croft remembers that whenever projectionist

Ron Webb knew his wife was in the auditorium, he used to put on 'You're the Cream in My Coffee'. Then came the musicals, **Evergreen** (1934) with Jessie Matthews being a great favourite of Sheila Bycroft and featuring numbers like 'Dancing On the Ceiling' by Rodgers and Hart.

Amy Dulake fondly recalls being taken by her mum and dad to see the English heart-throb Dirk Bogarde in **Campbell's Kingdom** (1957), and remembers the smallest audience the Kinema has ever seen, when only one young man turned up for a matinee of **Day of the Triffids** (1962) in which almost everyone in the world is blinded by meteorites prior to being taken over by intelligent plants. Amongst Amy's favourite films, however, are **Mame** (1974) with Lucille Ball and **The Wrong Box** (1966), a Bryan Forbes film with Ralph Richardson, and a host of stars including Mr Forbes' own wife Nanette Newman. In James Green's early years Amy remembers being given all the horror films to project, while Sheila Bycroft seemed to get all the sex films!

During the mid to late '70s, around a hundred bikers with all their leather gear and helmets came regularly on Sundays, parking in the old bike sheds to the side of the car park, and were always ravenous, having been out all day at Cadwell Park. The Dulake family decided to provide wrapped sandwiches which were greatly appreciated and which always disappeared 'like snow before the sun'!

We must not forget the amateur theatricals which took place for so many years on the Kinema stage. The Woodhall Spa Amateur Dramatic Society, in which Major S. V. Hotchkin took part, transferred at least one production to the stage of the Lincoln Theatre Royal. The play 'Interference' by Roland Pertwee and Harold Dearden, was one of these, and the film version was screened in the Kinema in October 1930, almost six months after the play. Captain Allport remarked in his press advert for the film 'You saw the amateurs! Now see the film!!' – a rather double-edged remark. The Tea House in the Woods sold tickets for the play.

On one level, the Kinema is made of brick, plaster and wood, but for most of those who love it, it is made of memories. When the popular radio programme 'Down Your Way' featured Woodhall Spa in 1976,

Brian Johnston came inside the Kinema and asked Sheila Bycroft to choose her favourite piece of music. She said it had to be Joan Regan singing 'When I Grow Too Old to Dream'. Many of the service men who flocked to those wartime matinees never had the chance to grow old or dream, but Noel Allport's Kinema gave them their last hours of pleasure. Perhaps that is why Mrs Webb remembered many years later, and with a lump in her throat, that some of those young men used to file in past her paybox and greet her with a cheery "Hello Beautiful".

THE END

# Appendix i

## Specification of the Compton Kinestra Organ

by David Hill, who designed the new specification when the installation was begun.

To date there have been no changes.

| PEDAL | |
|---|---|
| Acoustic Bass | 32 |
| Tuba | 16 |
| Tibia | 16 |
| Clarinet | 16 |
| Tuba | 8 |
| Diapason | 8 |
| Tibia | 8 |
| Violin | 8 |
| Tibia | 4 |
| Piano | 8 |
| Crash Cymbal | |
| Bass Drum Tap F | |
| Drum Roll (Bass) | |
| Cymbal | |
| Snare Drum | |
| Tolling Bell | |
| Triangle | |
| Accompaniment to Pedal | |
| Great To Pedal | |
| 2 Combination Pistons (Toe) | |
| Sound Effects on Toe Pistons | |
| Cymbal | |
| Birds 1 | |
| Birds 2 | |
| Train Whistle | |
| Door Bell | |
| Siren | |
| Klaxon | |
| Fire Gong | |
| Boat Whistle | |

| GREAT | |
|---|---|
| Tuba | |
| Diapason | 16 |
| Tibia | 16 |
| Clarinet | 16 |
| Tuba | 16 |
| Diapason | 8 |
| Vox Humana | 8 |
| Clarinet | 8 |
| Viole D'Orchestre | 8 |
| Viole Celeste | 8 |
| Flute | 8 |
| Clarion | 8 |
| Diapason | 4 |
| Tibia | 4 |
| Flute | 4 |
| Twelfth | $2^{2}/_{3}$ |
| Piccolo | 2 |
| Flautina | 2 |
| Tierce | $1^{3}/_{5}$ |
| Piano | 8 |
| Glockenspiel | 4 |
| Reiterator (Glock) | |
| Xylophone | 4 |
| Chimes | |
| Muted Chimes | |
| Octave Coupler | |
| 6 Combination Pistons | |

| ACCOMPANIMENT | | SOLO | |
|---|---|---|---|
| Vox Humana | 16 | Tuba | 16 |
| Viole | 16 | Tibia | 16 |
| Tuba | 8 | Tuba | 8 |
| Diapason | 8 | Diapason | 8 |
| Tibia | 8 | Tibia | 8 |
| Vox Humana | 8 | Vox Humana | 8 |
| Clarinet | 8 | Cello | 8 |
| Violin | 8 | Tuba | 4 |
| Viole Celeste | 8 | Tibia | 4 |
| Flute | 8 | Piano | 8 |
| Diapason | 4 | Glockenspiel | 4 |
| Tibia | 4 | Xylophone | 4 |
| Vox Humana | 4 | Chimes | |
| Violin | 4 | Octave Coupler | |
| Viole Celeste | 4 | Great to Solo Suboct. | 16 |
| Flute | 4 | Great to Solo | 8 |
| Snare Drum Tap | | Great to Solo Octave | 4 |
| Snare Drum Roll | | Great to Solo Tenth | 3 1/5 |
| Tom Tom | | Great to Solo Twelfth | 2 2/5 |
| Castanets | | | |
| Jingles | | | |
| Tambourine | | **TREMULANTS** | |
| Block | | Tuba | |
| Triangle | | Viole Celeste, Diapason, Clarinet | |
| Sand Block | | Vox Humana | |
| Octave Coupler | | Tibia | |
| Great Suboctave to Accomp.2nd | | Flute, Violin | |
| Great To Accomp. 2nd | | | |

2 Balance Swell Pedals
General Crescendo Pedal
Piano Sustain Toe Piston
Setter Piston
Double Touch Cancel to each Dept
Voltmeter for Action
Swell & Crescendo Indicators
Selector Switch for Memories 1 & 2

A Krummet is also available which may be fitted in place of the Clarinet, to give a brighter sound.

# Appendix ii
## The Projection Equipment
a note by James Green, including piano and organ information.

In 1922 there was no National Grid to carry electricity around the country and ultimately to the consumer's property. Towns and cities had their own 'electric company' which provided electricity in an assortment of voltages and in either a.c. or d.c. (alternating current or direct current). These small concerns were all nationalised and the 'grid' was formed in the early part of the 1930s.

When excavations and footings were being dug for Kinema extensions in 1994 cables were unearthed which appeared to connect the Kinema to the Spa Baths. These were not of any great size but would be sufficient to carry enough current for lighting, and run a small electric motor.

When the Kinema opened in September 1922, using rear-projection method, the projector used was an American 'Powers No 6'. A handle was fitted for turning over the mechanism while threading the film, and possibly to run up to speed before an electric motor was switched on. This would then run at a constant speed of 16 f.p.s. (frames per second). The projector was fitted with square top and bottom spool boxes which contained the 35mm nitrate film and would hold a spool containing a maximum of 2000 feet of film which would run for app. 23 minutes. The projector and arc lamp stood on a 'X' iron stand, very popular with machines made at that time. An external three blade shutter extrudes from the front of the mechanism. The Powers No 6 is on display in the Kinema foyer. And an illustration is included in this book.

The light source for projecting the film to the screen is not definitely known, but if the thickness of the unearthed cables is any indication it was not carbon arc, as they were not of the size required to pass the high current. As far as we know there was no generator fitted at that time so the illuminant was probably lime light. A pastille of lime was fitted to the lime pin or jet stage, the lime light jet has a mixing chamber into which oxygen and acetylene are led throughout their respective cylinder regulators, into the mixing chamber. Both gases form into a highly explosive mixture before they are blown out of the jet nozzle. Light emitting from the lime can then be focused by condenser lens to the projector 'gate'. Projection room fires were quite common in the early days of cinema with nitrate film (the base of which is nitro-glycerine) acetylene gas and oxygen for light source, acetone for film repairs – quite a volatile cocktail.

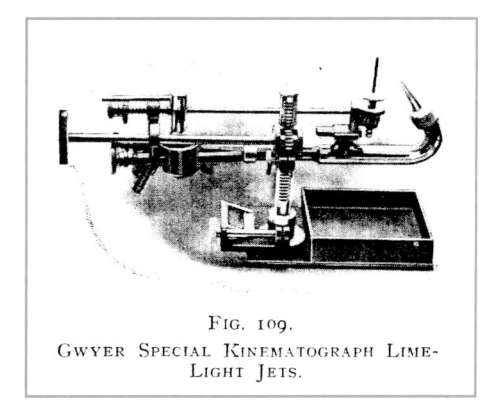

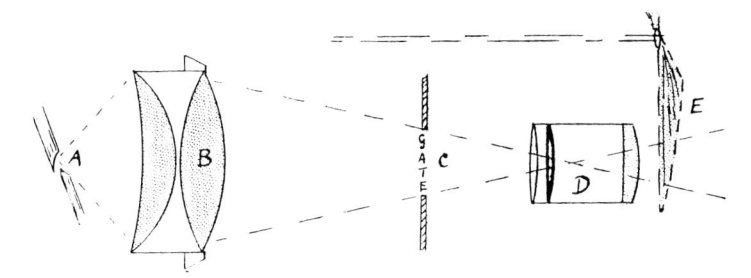

FIG. 109.
GWYER SPECIAL KINEMATOGRAPH LIME-LIGHT JETS.

FIG. 116. How a condenser converges light through the objective.

The first equipment change saw Kalee 7s installed, manufactured by A. Kershaw of Leeds, once again a silent projector, a pair of these would be installed to give continuity to the films. Carbon arc lamps would have replaced lime light ones, and we know that Gyrotone Sound On Disc was fitted to the projectors, giving synchronised sound, a 16 inch Panatrope (disc) from this very short period is on display in the foyer. Not long after sound on film apparatus was fitted to the projectors in the form of Gyrotone 'pull through' sound heads.

With the coming of sound the film speed was increased to 24 f.p.s.. Kalee 8s replaced the 7s during the 1940s.

The next equipment change was in the late 1940s. A pair of brand new Walturdaw 5 projectors (of Erneman design) with water cooled gates were fitted with Zeiss Ikon 'pull through' sound heads, and Mr W. Cooper's plate rectifier and dual amplifier completed this refit. New Hanley arc lamps would follow, also supplied by Walturdaw.

## APPENDIX II

This equipment was removed in 1978 when it was becoming increasingly difficult to get spare parts, and Kalee 12 projectors were installed, on Western Electric 'universal' sound bases. A three phase 'Ecwelite' Mercury arc rectifier replaced the singe phase plate rectifier, and the Kinema was then fitted with a British Acoustic S20 sound amplifier. 'Autoarc' arc lamps were fitted to each machine, these being the latest in carbon arc technology where positive and negative carbons were fed as required and controlled by photo-electric cells and accompanying electronic technology.

In 1984 the projection room was completely re-vamped using one Kalee 21 projector with '83' sound head, stand and Xenon arc lamp with T. and R. rectifier. Up until now the projectors beamed their picture onto the back of the translucent screen, the picture being reversed for rear projection by turning the film 180 degrees before it passed through the gate, this meant there had to be modifications to sound heads for scanning the sound track on the opposite side to normal. Now, with the projector parallel to the screen, the image is reversed by using a front silvered mirror. Supplying the projector with film is a Westrex Tower, a system which can hold 14,000 feet of film for continuous showing through one projector, this is double sided and can be revolved as required for showing or rewinding. New projection lenses were acquired for Wide Screen and Cinemascope ratios.

1998 saw the sound system upgraded to Dolby 5 Track Surround Sound, this was supplied and fitted by Omnex of Manchester, and the first film it was used on was **Star Wars Episode 1**.

Kinema Too is equipped with a Kalee 21 projector and 83 sound head, Xenon lamp house, Westrex Tower and also has Dolby 5 Track Surround Sound.

### Organ information:
Made in 1927, it was the first console to be fitted with double-touch cancelling to the stop tabs. Christie Music Transmission system is used throughout, where the digital signals are multiplexed from the console to the main relay through a single core screened cable. A solid state capture system is used for all pistons and has provision for two memories.

The organ is wind powered by three blowers using 7.5kw of electricity.

**Piano information:**
On the left of the stage is a Phantom piano, which plays, should the organist desire, from the console, this is a Broadwood 'Barless' 6 foot 6inch grand piano originally built as a player piano in 1910 fully restored and converted to Electro pneumatic action at the Kinema.

The piano on the right of the stage is a fully restored Steck Duo-Art reproducing grand piano, made to order for a doctor in Birmingham in 1932, the piano plays faithfully from paper rolls as recorded by the pianist with all expressions and nuances.

Both pianos are of the 'moving key' variety which intrigue and fascinate.

## About the author

*Photo courtesy of Lincolnshire Today*

**Edward Mayor** is a freelance artist and writer living in Woodhall Spa with his partner Jonathan and their two border terriers Jessie and Rosie. Known locally as 'the man on the tricycle with the two dogs', he has written best-selling books about Woodhall Spa's Petwood Hotel and Duncan Grant's murals in Lincoln Cathedral. He has known the Kinema for almost fifty years, and watched Disney films while seated in its deck chairs, which vanished in the 1950's.